D1279664

Wildlife Conservationist

Trudi Strain Trueit

Cavendish Square

New York

Published in 2014 by Cavendish Square Publishing, LLC
303 Park Avenue South, Suite 1247, New York, NY 10010

First Edition

Website: cavendishsq.com

This publication represents the opinions and views of the author based on his or her personal experience, knowledge, and research. The information in this book serves as a general guide only. The author and publisher have used their best efforts in preparing this book and disclaim liability rising directly or indirectly from the use and application of this book.

CPSIA Compliance Information: Batch #WW14CSQ

All websites were available and accurate when this book was sent to press.

Library of Congress Cataloging-in-Publication Data

Wildlife conservationist / by Trudi Strain Trueit.
p. cm. — (Careers with animals)
Includes index.
ISBN 978-1-62712-467-6 (hardcover) ISBN 978-1-62712-468-3 (paperback) ISBN 978-1-62712-469-0 (ebook)
1. Environmental protection — Vocational guidance — Juvenile literature. 2. Environmental protection — Juvenile literature. I. Trueit, Trudi Strain. II. Title.
TD170 .M54 T74 2014
333.7—dc23

Editorial Director: Dean Miller
Senior Editor: Peter Mavrikis
Copy Editor: Cynthia Roby
Art Director: Jeffrey Talbot
Designer: Amy Greenan
Photo Researcher: Julie Alissi, J8 Media
Production Manager: Jennifer Ryder-Talbot
Production Editor: Andrew Coddington

Printed in the United States of America

CONTENTS

ONE

Defenders of Life

"**W**hen I was a kid, I saw a picture of a whooping crane in a bird field guide book. And I thought to myself, 'I'll never see one of these,'" laughs Dr. John French. The wildlife conservationist can smile about it now because not only does he see these **endangered** birds *every* day, he goes to extraordinary lengths to help save them!

As research manager at the U.S. Geological Survey's Patuxent Research Center in Maryland, Dr. French leads a captive whooping crane breeding program with a long history. The program began back in the late 1960s when the birds were first listed as endangered by the U.S. Fish and Wildlife Service. The goal was, and is, to bring the tallest bird in North America—the whooping crane reaches 5 feet (1.5 m) in height—back from the brink of **extinction**. Trying to coax nature along, however, is a delicate process. Scientists must carefully match the whooping cranes that are housed at the center for compatibility. This can mean months or even years of "bird dating," or putting different males in pens on each side of a penned female to see which she prefers.

Whoopers in the wild typically lay a clutch of two eggs but raise only the first chick that hatches (the birds at Patuxent tend to lay more than two eggs). Dr. French and his team collect all the additional eggs. Initially, the

(Opposite) Pictured here in the wetlands, the whooping crane was declared endangered in 1967.

eggs are incubated by surrogate sandhill cranes. When they are within a few days of hatching, the eggs are moved to an incubating machine and tended by people. From the moment a whooper chick cracks its shell, it is cared for by a conservationist wearing a white poncho and matching hood and holding a crane-head puppet. The costumed "parent" uses the puppet to teach chicks to eat, drink, forage, and exercise. "When we raise chicks by hand, the whole point of the costume is to hide the human form so the chicks don't grow up to become accustomed to humans," explains Dr. French. "Wearing the costume is brutal but necessary. It's hot in there!" The young chicks also are taught to follow their faux parent as he/she drives an ultralight aircraft on the grass. In a couple of months, the chicks are driven by truck to Wisconsin and unloaded. As before, the chicks trail the ultralight as it rides along the

A baby whooping crane mimics its costumed parent as it prepares for its first flight. Zoo employee Anita Vincent helps the bird with an exercise to strengthen its pectorals, which control the wings.

Whooping cranes thrive on open tidal marsh. Densely wooded areas don't allow them to elude predators.

ground. This time, however, there is a pilot inside the crane costume. Soon, the ultralight takes off! The chicks spread their massive wings and follow their parent skyward to begin a 1,200-mile (1,930 km) journey to Florida for their first migration. "It's just a lovely sight to see them fly," says Dr. French. "It's even more affecting to see the birds in subsequent years, migrating all on their own."

The Patuxent Research Center is part of the Whooping Crane Eastern Partnership, a group of state and federal agencies and private conservation groups dedicated to helping these birds rebound. Their painstaking work is paying off. In 1942, there were just sixteen wild whooping cranes left in North America. People hunting them for their plumes and eggs, along with human development of their shoreline habitats, nearly destroyed them. Today, whooping cranes number close to 600 in the wild and in captivity. "All the birds that are alive today derive from that one flock of sixteen birds in 1942," explains Dr. French. "The goal is to get the population numbers up so the birds can be down-listed from endangered to **threatened** and then finally off the [U.S. Fish and Wildlife Service's] species list entirely. It's a positive and hopeful project. But we still have a long way to go."

The Right Thing to Do

Across the globe, wildlife conservationists work to protect and preserve many of Earth's plant and animal **species**. This book focuses on those who advocate for animals and spend much of their time around or with them. Animal conservationists typically enjoy being outside. As kids, they often spent their spare time hiking, boating, camping, beachcombing, or doing other fun outdoor activities. Their appreciation of nature may have led them to clean a park, plant a school or community garden, or help restore a habitat. Conservationists also tend to be big animal lovers. While in middle and high school, many enjoyed volunteering at zoos, wildlife rehabilitation centers, veterinary clinics, kennels, animal shelters, or horse stables. Dr. John French found a way to combine both interests. In high school, he worked summers for the Massachusetts Audobon Society, traveling by boat to New England's outer islands to help band birds for identification. "I didn't realize then that it would be my future," he says. "It was just a happy time."

Most conservationists attended college to earn a bachelor's degree and one or more advanced degrees, such as a master's or doctorate. Many concentrated their studies in the sciences. Some chose an area within the science of **biology**, such as **ecology**, **zoology**, **marine biology**, or **genetics**.

Women Take a Stand

In the late nineteenth century, Boston society ladies Harriet Hemenway and her cousin Minna Hall were outraged by a trend in women's fashion sweeping the United States and Europe: hats decorated with real feathers and dead birds. A single hat might be adorned with egret plumes, owl heads, sparrow wings, and whole hummingbirds. The long, white mating head feathers of the great and snowy egret were so valuable— sometimes selling for up to five times the price of gold—plume hunters nearly wiped out these bird populations on the Atlantic seaboard. Shocked by descriptions in the press of hunters massacring nesting egrets, Hemenway and Hall founded the Massachusetts Audubon Society in 1896. The organization's mission to protect birds spread across the country. The Boston cousins and other conservationists helped to get laws passed making it illegal to kill shorebirds, but not before tens of millions of egrets, herons, gulls, cranes, terns, and other birds lost their lives in the name of fashion.

Call of the Wild

Is a career in wildlife conservation calling you? It might be if you answer "yes" to most of these questions:

- Do you have a passion for wanting to help wild animals and protect their habitats?
- Are you an active person who loves outdoor activities, such as hiking, mountain climbing, boating, or scuba diving?
- Are you primarily interested in studying the sciences, and can you earn top grades in these classes?
- Are you willing to spend significant time in college (six years or more) studying and performing research in an area of wildlife conservation that interests you?
- Are you a self-starter, meaning can you work independently on a project without substantial guidance from others?
- Are you a "people person" with strong writing and public speaking skills?
- Would you like a job that involves travel and perhaps living in unsettled areas that may not have all the comforts of home?

Wardens from Kenya Wildlife Service examine tusks and skins recovered from poachers. In 2013, the organization reported the loss of 384 elephants—the highest ever recorded loss in a single year.

Others selected to study animal sciences and perhaps animal behavior or agriculture. Still others preferred wildlife management or wildlife conservation.

A career in wildlife conservation may include studying animals, saving and restoring habitats, rescuing orphaned or injured wildlife, working on breeding and reintroduction of species programs, educating the public, and fundraising. For some, the job involves extensive travel or living in another country. Far from home, they may endure rough conditions in remote locations. Harsh weather, disease, animal attacks, and threats from **poachers** are some of the obstacles that may hinder their work.

So why do people devote their lives to such a demanding career? It may be the realization that every life form has a role to play in an ecosystem. Like a line of falling dominoes, the more species we lose, the more we upset the balance of nature and, ultimately, put our own survival in peril. "The last word in ignorance is the man who says of an animal or plant, 'What good is it?'" wrote forester and conservationist Aldo Leopold (1887–1948), who laid the foundation for wildlife management in the United States. "To keep every cog and wheel is the first precaution of intelligent tinkering."

Conservationists are also inspired by their enthusiasm for animals and nature, and the desire to see that neither is harmed. In 1962, ecologist and writer for the U.S. Fish and Wildlife Service (FWS) Rachel Carson published *Silent Spring*, a book warning that pesticide use by humans was causing significant damage to songbirds and other wildlife (the title referred to the possibility of a world without birds). Carson took a great deal of heat from chemical companies and government officials for her revelations, but the public listened. A new era of environmental awareness was born. The movement resulted in the 1973 Endangered Species Act, a law providing for the protection and conservation of the nation's threatened and endangered plants and animals and their habitats. Finally, conservation is a way for those who care about the future of our planet to make amends for the past. "It feels like the right thing for me to do, personally, to redress the environmental damage that's caused by human activities," reveals Dr. John French. "Humans often seem themselves outside of nature. Perhaps we would do things differently if we saw the connection." Conservationists not only see the connection but are driven to strengthen the bond.

(Opposite) Kowanyama, in the Yir-Yoront language, means "the place of many waters." In good condition, the wetlands in this region of Australia include freshwater lakes, sand plains, beach ridges, swamps, lakes, and intertidal flats.

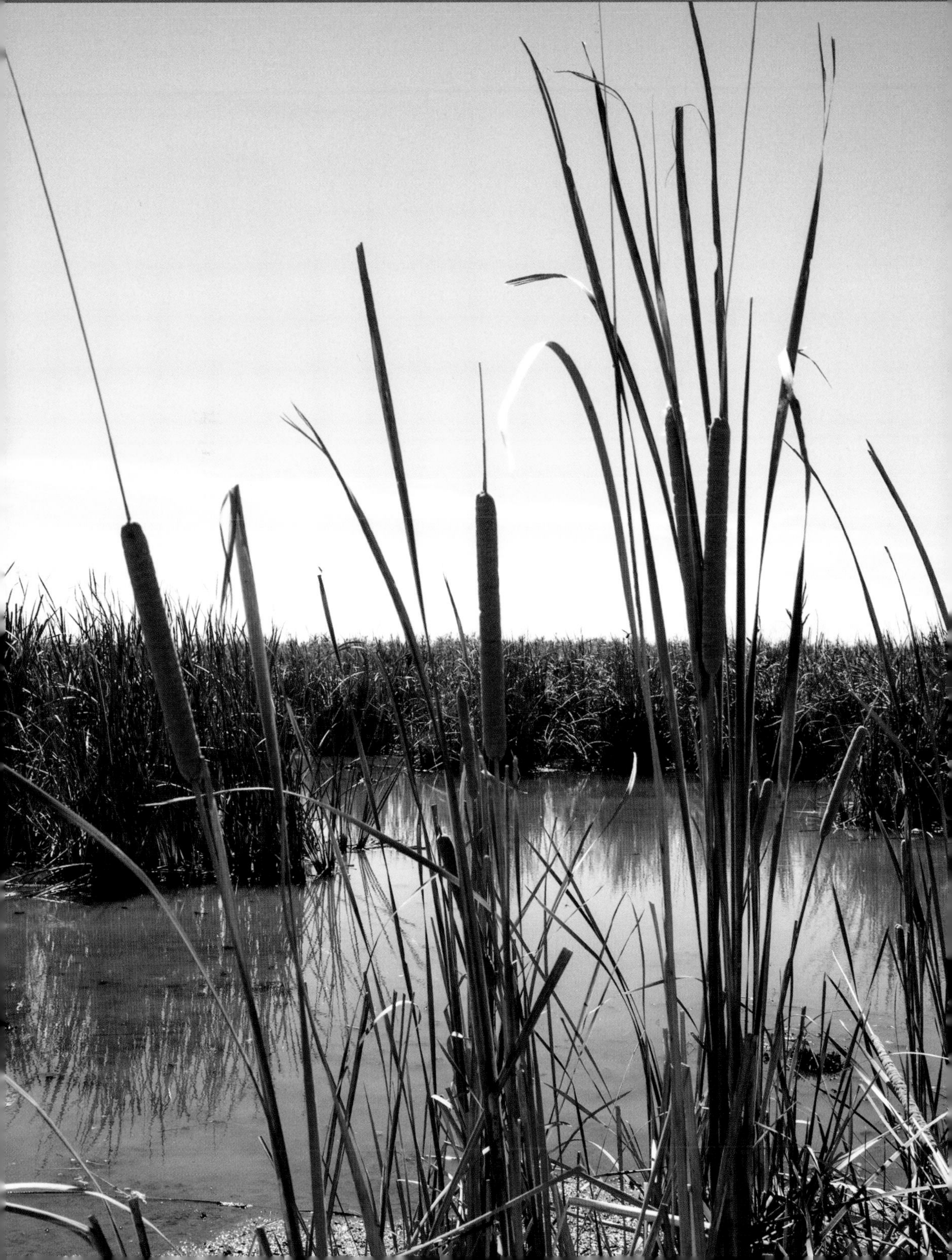

TWO

The Power of Knowledge

Anyone may participate in conservation efforts. But if you want to make it your life's work, plan on attending college to earn a bachelor's degree. Also, many employers prefer, and some jobs require, applicants to have one or more advanced college degrees, such as a master's and/or a doctorate (PhD). The Wildlife Society reports about one-third of those with bachelor's degrees are immediately successful right out of school in finding a job in the wildlife field. Those with master's degrees do better, with two-thirds obtaining positions upon graduation. Generally, it takes about four years to earn a bachelor's degree, about two years for a masters, and an additional three to seven for a PhD. Those interested in wildlife veterinary medicine will attend veterinary college following completion of their bachelors. (For further information on veterinarian school, read *Veterinarian* in the Careers with Animals series).

Why so much education? Advanced degree curriculums teach students skills that are essential to conservation work. In a graduate program, a student learns how to conduct in-depth research, analyze data, make conclusions, and present the findings. Additionally, these programs demand

(Opposite) A group of elementary school students study a bearded dragon, a type of lizard that originates in Australia.

A Summer Adventure

Would you like to help monitor turtle nesting sites or learn how to band geese? If you're between the ages of 15 and 18, you're eligible to apply for the Youth Conservation Corps (YCC), a government-sponsored summer work program that hires teens for various conservation projects across the country. Students work full-time (40 hours per week) in the field under the supervision of professionals for eight to ten weeks. Pay is minimum wage. Established in 1970, YCC is a joint effort of the U.S. Fish and Wildlife Service, the National Park Service, the U.S. Forest Service, and the Bureau of Land Management. Log on to the website of any of these agencies to find out about projects going on in your area and apply to the program.

a student devote significant time to studying, observing, and sometimes coming into contact with a particular species of animal. In the next chapter, you'll discover how conservationists put these abilities to use on the job.

Get a Head Start

To prepare for a conservation career, middle and high school students are advised to focus their studies on the sciences, math, and social studies. "You need to have a good background in science," says Carey Stanton, senior director of education with National Wildlife Federation. "Conservation needs to be based on sound science, not just on emotions and passion. You are not going to be able to do what's best for a species and for people if you aren't basing it on fact." Academic advisors say a solid science curriculum should include classes in biology, earth science, chemistry, and physics. Take math every year, studying algebra, geometry, precalculus, calculus, and statistics. In the area of social studies, world history, geography, and global issues are advised. Communication arts classes are also highly recommended because conservationists must write articles and reports, present their work orally, and educate the public. "It's important to have strong communication skills in public speaking as well as writing so you can clearly convey your message," says Stanton. Learning a foreign language is also wise. Conservationists work on every continent on Earth, in countries such as China, Russia, Kenya, Turkey, Mexico, and Brazil. Academic counselors suggest students enroll in advanced placement (AP) courses whenever possible. They should strive to earn a B-average, or 3.0 or above grade-point average, in their classes.

To expand skills, build confidence, and learn to work cooperatively, become active in clubs at your school. Find those that revolve around science, math, leadership, community service, and conservation. If you don't have a conservation or environmental club at your school, why not start one? It's a great way to begin making a difference right where you are. From bullfrogs to bald eagles, the survival of a species depends on its environment. Your club could spearhead a project to restore a habitat, clean a beach or wetland area, or hold a fundraiser to benefit a conservation organization. Outside of school, explore conservation through 4-H Youth Development, Boy Scouts, and Girl Scouts. Many government and **nonprofit** conservation organizations offer summer jobs, camps, or volunteer programs for teens, among them the U.S. Fish and Wildlife Service, The Nature Conservancy, the Jane Goodall Institute, and the National Audubon Society. Check with your favorite conservation group to see what opportunities they offer for students.

Is there an animal or area of wildlife that fascinates you? Perhaps you are interested in ornithology (birds), herpetology (reptiles and amphibians), ichthyology (fish), marine animals, or mammals. Or maybe you aren't sure yet about a specialty. Read books, watch DVDs, and take classes to explore the possibilities. Visit zoos, aquariums, wildlife sanctuaries, and marine mammal facilities. Many of these places offer summer camps and classes where you can learn about conservation and possibly see threatened or endangered species up close! Experience is also a plus. Volunteer at a wildlife rehabilitation center, wildlife sanctuary, fish hatchery, veterinary clinic,

kennel, horse stable, or animal shelter. While the National Wildlife Federation's Carey Stanton was in high school and college, she worked at a local zoo. "I grew up reading *Ranger Rick* magazine and knowing I wanted to work for National

Students from Richvale and Chico's Sierra View elementary schools discover a nest of duck eggs.

Chemistry is a recommended course for wildlife conservationist hopefuls. The subject places students in an excellent position to choose from a wide variety of useful, interesting, and rewarding careers.

Wildlife Federation," she says. "Now I do!" Keep a journal of your work experience and log the hours you serve (keep it up to date as you go through college). Your journal will come in handy when you apply to graduate schools or veterinary colleges.

College Bound

Aspiring conservationists should research colleges and universities to find a school with respected science and math programs. It should also have a stellar reputation for research. Look for a school that can connect you with

Paying Your Way

The National Center for Education Statistics reports more than 70 percent of graduate students in the United States receive financial aid to help meet their college expenses. In exchange for conducting research, teaching classes, assisting faculty, and other duties, a student may receive various forms of compensation. He/she may earn a salary, called a stipend (STY-pend), health insurance, and/or free tuition. A student may also receive financial assistance from an employer, nonprofit organization, or student loan program. Federal and private fellowships, awards, grants, and scholarships are also available. However, to remain eligible to receive these funds, which do not need to be repaid, schools typically require students to maintain a certain GPA, often a B-average (3.0).

an array of volunteer opportunities, **internships**, and study abroad programs in the area of wildlife conservation. This path is key, because it's not uncommon for conservation employers to hire new employees from their pool of volunteers or interns. Ask about a conservation club or other on-campus efforts in which you can become involved. Clubs are a great way for students to get hands-on experience helping a species, working with local conservation groups, doing research, and educating the public. At the University of California, Davis, students may join the campus chapter of Wildlife Society or other student-run conservation clubs such as Wild Campus and Wild Forces.

As you are considering colleges for your undergraduate studies, it's wise to be thinking about where you may want to do your graduate work. Some schools offer joint programs that allow students to earn two degrees simultaneously (dual-degree programs), such as a bachelors and masters, or masters and doctorate. Don't expect, however, a joint program to shave significant time off your education. It's not necessary to earn all your degrees at the same school. Some academic counselors even advise against it. They say potential employers are most impressed with applicants who have widened their circle of experience and education by earning their degrees at different schools. In the end, you should choose a program based on its merits and how it meshes with your career goals.

To earn a bachelor's degree, students usually choose a major, or a particular area of study. Majors common among those in the conservation field are the sciences, such as general biology, zoology, ecology, genetics, animal science, agriculture, wildlife conservation, and wildlife management. But you may choose to study any science that appeals to you. A strong science curriculum will cover cellular biology, anatomy, genetics, physiology, chemistry, and physics. Ornithology, ichthyology, entomology, and other classes that focus on specific groups of animals should be included as well. Students are advised to maintain a B-average, or 3.0 or above grade-point average. Top grades will be an advantage when applying to graduate schools or looking for an entry-level job. Upon receiving their bachelor's degree, many students will prepare for graduate school. Students may choose to pursue a masters, a PhD, or both (either simultaneously or in succession). Some schools require a student to have a masters before earning a PhD, while others do not. Those applying to graduate school must take the General Record Examination (GRE). This four-hour computer-based test measures critical reasoning, reading comprehension, writing skills, and basic math knowledge. Academic advisors say students can, and should, apply to more than one graduate school. Each has its own application requirements and process, but generally, students will submit the following:

- A written application, which includes selecting a master's program of study, such as biology or conservation
- Statement of Purpose: a short personal essay detailing why the student wants to pursue graduate studies and his/her career goals
- Three letters of recommendation from professors, advisors, or professionals that have supervised the student in a volunteer, internship, or work capacity
- Résumé or details of prior work and internship experience
- Official undergraduate transcripts
- GRE scores
- Application fee

Many schools require students to apply online. Completed applications are usually reviewed by an admissions committee within each graduate department. They meet once or twice per year to decide which students to accept. At some schools, students are asked to appear before the committee for an interview. Students are informed of their acceptance by letter or e-mail and may accept or decline the offer.

Let's Get Ready to Research!

After receiving a bachelor's degree, some students continue their education and enroll in a graduate program. Others find employment first and return to school at a later date to pursue one or more advanced degrees. They may attend school full or part-time, depending on time and finances.

In a master's degree program, students take courses, teach classes, and assist with research in the lab. In addition, they complete a **thesis**, or independent, original research project. Some schools offer a non-thesis option, which substitutes coursework for research. A student interested in wildlife conservation might do a thesis on a specific animal's behavior, physical characteristic, or a threat that puts a species in jeopardy. Under the watchful eye of a faculty advisor or committee, a student spends about two years on a thesis: creating and submitting a proposal for a theme, conducting research, collecting data, and analyzing findings. At the conclusion of the project, he/she completes a written report detailing the research and results. The report is then submitted to a graduate studies committee made up of the student's advisor and other faculty members. In addition, the student delivers

Students in a Jersey City chemistry lab use microscopes to perform experiments.

an oral presentation in front of the committee, faculty, students, and other guests. This is called a thesis defense. The student presents his/her thesis and answers questions, or defends it. If the committee is satisfied that a student has met the goals for completing the thesis, it grants approval for graduation. Students who choose a non-thesis track must pass a written examination in order to graduate.

The process of earning a PhD, also called a doctorate, is similar to that of a master's program. However, the program is longer and the research more in-depth. PhD candidates spend, on average, about five years earning their degree. Because the studies can be so time consuming, it's not uncommon for conservationists to return to school to get their PhD after being in the field for a number of years. Many continue in their jobs (or cut back to part time) while enrolled in their degree studies. The U.S. Department of Education's National Center for Education Statistics reports that about half of all doctoral candidates attend school part time. Doctoral students are usually required to take courses, teach undergraduate classes (for one or more years), and pass a qualifying exam (often in the second year). They must also complete an original research project, called a thesis or dissertation. The project requires a student to focus on a topic and do extensive research. For those pursuing a career in wildlife conservation it can be an opportunity to thoroughly study behaviors, characteristics, or habitats of a particular animal in the wild. As with masters programs, PhD candidates must submit their dissertation in writing, as well as present and defend it in public.

By the time someone earns a PhD, he or she will have spent years studying a species and will be considered an expert in his or her field. Yet, those who are committed to protecting animals know there is always more to learn. For them, the journey has just begun.

(Opposite) A view from the Kungsleden trails of the wetlands in the Tärnasjön area, Vindelfjällen. With an area of 1.35 million acres (550,000 hectares), Vindelfjällen is one of largest conservation areas in Europe.

THREE

Saving a Species

Wildlife conservationists may put their education, skills, and passion to work for any number of employers. Many are hired by state or federal government agencies, such as the U.S. Fish and Wildlife Service, the U.S. Geological Survey, or the Department of Agriculture. Some work for nonprofit conservation groups, such as National Wildlife Federation, World Wildlife Fund, Sea Turtle Conservancy, or Cheetah Conservation Fund. Others are employed by private research facilities, university research centers, aquariums, or zoos.

It's not uncommon for several different organizations, say, a government agency, nonprofit group, and zoo, to come together and work cooperatively on a project. But how do these conservationists discover what needs to be done? And how do they accomplish it? Just what *does* it take to save a species?

Quest of Discovery

Most conservation organizations actively study the animals for which they advocate. They do this to learn as much as they can about an animal's characteristics, behavior, and habitat needs. They also study a species in its natural environment to identify threats to its survival—threats that are frequently caused by humans. Habitat loss (often due to development,

(Opposite) An ornithologist (one who studies birds) in Papua, New Guinea, carefully removes a mid-mountain berrypecker from a mist net.

This harpy eagle is being carried by Alexander Blanco through the swamp to dry ground in Ecuador's Amazon rain forest. Despite it being legendary, only a few people have seen a harpy eagle in the wild.

Conservation Nation

Tasked with protecting and conserving the country's natural resources, the U.S. Fish and Wildlife Service (FWS) employs thousands of conservation professionals. Headquartered in Washington DC, FWS has seven regional offices and nearly 700 field units spanning from Alaska to Guam to Puerto Rico. FWS wildlife biologists may be involved in animal tagging and tracking projects, monitoring waterfowl migrations, taking population surveys, restoring habitats, or reintroducing endangered species. Entry-level biology jobs require a bachelor's degree in science or natural resources. The salary range is from $27,400 to $44,000, but you may be able to start at a higher level if your undergraduate grade point average is 3.0 or above, or if you have an advanced degree. More experienced wildlife biologists earn up to $78,000 per year.

A member of an expedition in the Foja Mountains records birdcalls. The Foja Mountains are located just north of the Mamberamo river basin in Papua, New Guinea.

logging, or farming), overfishing or hunting, animal-human conflict, and poaching pose the greatest risks to animals. Still, there are plenty of other dangers, such as climate change, predators, disease, pollution, and competition for food. Conservation groups employ **field research** scientists to gather firsthand information about a species, its habitat, and threats. Researchers generally have one or more advanced degrees in an area of science, such as biology, ecology, zoology, or marine biology. Ecologists explore how animals interact with their environment. They look at habitat requirements, food and water quality, climate, and pollution. Zoologists and biologists study animal characteristics and behaviors, such as feeding, breeding, disease, populations, habitats, and movement or migration. Marine biologists specialize in researching plants and animals in the ocean (saltwater environments).

The salaries of research scientists vary, depending upon duties, education, experience, and employer. The U.S. Department of Labor reports that in 2010, the average pay for wildlife zoologists and biologists was more than

A researcher studies a colony of penguins in their habitat.
(Opposite) A one-day-old baby king cobra under the observation of Indian reptile conservationist Mohammed Anees.

$57,000 per year. The bottom 10 percent on the pay scale earned less than $36,000 per year, while the top 10 percent made an annual salary of more than $93,000.

A researcher may need to travel in order to study and observe an animal in its natural habitat. This could mean heading to a remote part of the world, perhaps to the frigid Antarctic to watch emperor penguins raise their young or to the steamy rain forests of South America to view the nesting habits of macaws. A researcher may spend weeks, months, or even years in the field. He/she may live in a small village, hut, or tent. Duties may include observing behavior, counting populations, identifying threats, examining a habitat, and conducting experiments. In their work, researchers may also collect samples, such as animal hair or scat (animal droppings). To find scat, a researcher may follow an animal's tracks or use a detector dog that is trained to pick up the scent. Locating scat gives scientists clues about population levels and how animals move within their habitat. The researcher collects the scat and sends it to the genetics lab. Analysis will reveal information about an animal's nutrition, toxins, stress, and reproductive health. New technologies are now allowing geneticists to extract DNA from hair or scat to learn more about an animal's family tree and even estimate the size of a population in a particular area! If an animal is rare, not easily observed, or hunts at night, a researcher may set up **camera traps** at various locations. These digital cameras are activated by heat or motion (they do not actually trap an animal). When an animal approaches, the sensor picks up the movement or the body's heat signature and triggers a video or still camera. The researcher returns later to retrieve the data so it can be viewed on a computer and analyzed. From their fieldwork, researchers may uncover new or fascinating information about how a species lives, hunts, breeds, or moves. Sometimes, they even find a *new* species!

Close Contact

As part of their quest to learn about a species, scientists may briefly capture animals. A scientist may safely catch and release smaller animals on their own, such as frogs, fish, and birds. Larger animals, such as bears, lions, or elephants may require a team. Trapping animals may involve using snares, cages, or even nets dropped from helicopters. Sometimes, tracking dogs are used to locate an animal. A researcher shoots

A Keen Eye

Conservationists working in the field must be good observers and able to clearly articulate what they see in their notes, journals, and blogs. Here's a blog post from conservationist Sara Blackburn, whose work for the Mara Predator Project involves monitoring lions in and around Maasai Mara National Reserve in Kenya, Africa.

Thursday, June 17: Charm's New Arrivals

For some weeks now, Charm's been looking very full. And I don't think it's all down to her sharp eyes and teeth! For about a week, Charm has distanced herself from the rest of the pride and has been hunting and resting alone. Yesterday we found out why! Yesterday I found Charm hidden deep in Maternity Lugga. She had with her some tiny cubs, probably no more than a week old. Although I didn't manage to count them, it is thought that she has three cubs—this is actually the typical number for lionesses. Charm will keep her cubs hidden until they are old enough to follow her around comfortably. New mums are very secretive, and she will only spend fleeting moments with her sisters. If the pride move back to their home, Musiara Marsh, she may be forced to move the cubs. It's also up to Clawed and Romeo to protect the pride from any other males, as a turnover would be disastrous for the new cubs.

Sara

Wildlife officers tag a brown bear found wandering through a Denver neighborhood. The animal was tranquilized so it could be safely returned to its habitat in the wild.

the animal with a tranquilizing dart to **anesthetize** it. While the animal is unconscious, scientists may measure body or paw size, collect blood or tissue samples, or note other helpful data, such as age, sex, or identifying features. Sometimes a veterinarian accompanies the team to examine the animal's body and teeth, and check for illness or injury. Scientists may also attach an identification band, tag, or tracking device to the animal. A lightweight radio transmitter or Global Positioning System (GPS) receiver are typically used. Bears, elephants, and big cats are given collars. Birds are outfitted with backpacks. Sea turtles get small transmitters glued to their shells (these do

Thrills and Chills

Conservation fieldwork can make for an adventurous career. "I've climbed into bear dens to take measurements, tackled caribou calves by jumping off the skids of a moving helicopter, and caught molting oldsquaw ducks by herding them into underwater mists nets," reveals Dr. John Morton. But the job has its dangerous side, too. Wild animals are, of course, unpredictable. Dr. Morton has had a few close calls with bears. Once, he was charged by white-lipped peccaries (animals similar to pigs) deep in the upper Amazon forest in Ecuador and had to shoot. Extreme weather, disease, and poachers are among the other hazards conservationists in the field must be prepared to face.

A pack of angry Congo elephants close in on Joseph Sentongo, the warden in charge of Queen Elizabeth National Park. Some elephants fled to the calm region of western Uganda because of unrest brought on by the war in Congo.

not harm the turtle and will fall off after about a year). Once, while U.S. Fish and Wildlife biologist Dr. John Morton was collaring a 450-pound (200-kg) grizzly bear, she awoke! Fortunately, the anesthetic kicked in and she quickly fell back to sleep. Tracking devices allow conservationists to pinpoint an animal's location and follow its movements over time. It can reveal valuable information about how animals migrate, use their habitat, interact with each other, spend the winter, and choose where to raise their young.

Upon the completion of a project, research scientists share their discoveries with the world. It's customary to write a paper detailing all data, analyses, and findings. Researchers will also reveal the threats to a species by using their knowledge and expertise to offer strategies for dealing with these issues. Suggestions may include educating local citizens on the value of a species, restoring a habitat, changing laws to curb human development, or stepping up law enforcement to halt poaching. Researchers tend to be quite adamant about the importance of this part of their job. They may write articles and books, speak at conferences, conduct seminars, meet with government officials, and hold community forums—whatever is necessary to help people recognize that a species is in jeopardy. Their revelations spur the organizations they work for, and with luck, humanity, to take action before a species is lost forever.

Turning the Tide

Once the risk factors to a species have been identified and investigated, a conservation organization explores ways to combat them. To stop habitat destruction, a group may take legal action or appeal to a government for assistance. To protect an animal from poachers, it may patrol nesting sites or work closely with law enforcement. To keep local livestock ranchers from killing the wildlife they view as predators, a conservation group may provide education, guard dogs, or sturdier enclosures.

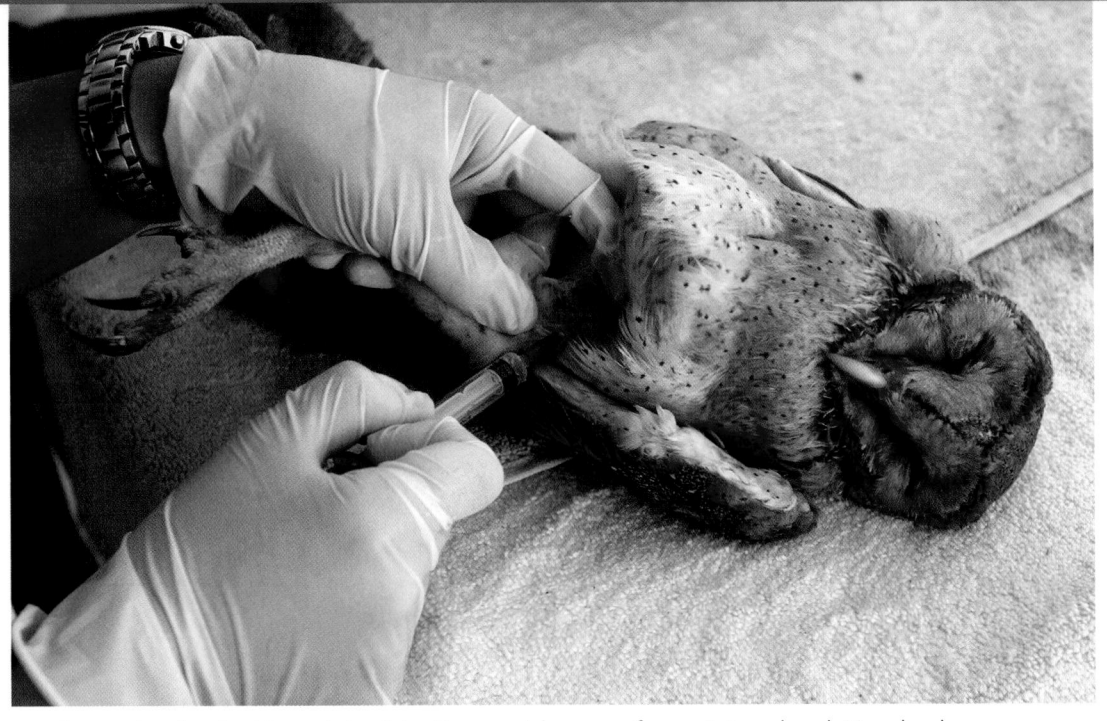

A veterinarian in Ahmadabad, India, provides care for an injured owl. Hundreds of birds lose their lives or become permanently disabled by flying into metal and glass-coated kite strings during Uttarayan, the annual kite festival.

(Opposite) Almost hunted to the brink of extinction, this pair of red wolf pups is being nurtured by a Fish and Wildlife Service worker.

A conservation organization may also be involved in directly helping animals. Some organizations rescue animals that have been injured or orphaned. Veterinarians, veterinarian technicians (nurses), and animal keepers tend to the animals until they are healthy or old enough to be released back into the wild. Sadly, sometimes an animal is too disabled to fend for itself and cannot be returned to its natural habitat. In these cases, it may be kept at a facility to use for breeding or educational purposes. A wildlife veterinarian oversees the diet, exercise, and health care of the animals. He/she provides routine medical exams, vaccinations, and dental care, and performs surgery as necessary. The salary of wildlife veterinarians varies from $60,000 to more than $100,000 per year, depending on experience, employer, duties, and location.

According to the U.S. Bureau of Labor Statistics, veterinarians, on average, earn an annual salary of about $82,000.

Breeding programs are another way conservation groups assist animal populations in recovering. Frequently, these programs are overseen by government conservation agencies that work in cooperation with a nonprofit group, research facility, or zoo. Animals are bred in captivity and their offspring are released into the wild when they are old enough to survive on their own. Sometimes scientists will remove eggs from a bird's nest, replace them with plastic eggs for the parent to brood, and incubate the real eggs by machine. This is done to keep predators and hunters from taking the eggs. The newly hatched chicks are then returned to their parents for rearing. Breeding programs have proved an effective way to bolster populations of species on the verge of extinction, including the bald eagle, California condor, and the whooping crane.

Rescued by SeaWorld San Diego Animal Care Team, this sea lion, discovered dehydrated and malnourished on a beach in Oceanside, California, suffered wounds to its left flipper.

In breeding programs, as well as in the wild, conservationists must work to protect diversity, or variety. When animal populations start to fall, they may inbreed and lose diversity. This makes each new generation more susceptible to deformity and disease, which leads to further decline in populations. Some conservation organizations employ geneticists at on-site labs (others send their samples out to labs). These scientists analyze animal blood, hair, and scat samples to find out more about the health and diversity of a population.

They may help oversee breeding programs and monitor wildlife populations in a particular area to ensure diversity. The pay for geneticists is similar to that of field biologists. According to the U.S. Department of Labor, salaries range from $35,000 to $93,000 per year, depending on education, experience, duties, and employer.

You've peered behind the scenes to see the extraordinary efforts that go into saving animals. Now it's time to meet the people who devote their lives to ensuring that thousands of threatened and endangered species have a future.

(Opposite) The sun sets over Ljubljana Marshes, a natural area of wetlands and peat bogs. The marsh boasts rare animal and vegetal species, and the remains of the prehistoric pile dwellings.

FOUR

Meet the Conservationists

D r. Laurie Marker has a passion for cheetahs and a message for humanity. "Cheetahs are running out of time in and outside national parks and reserves," she says. Wild cheetahs once roamed throughout Asia, Africa, and the Middle East. A century ago, their populations numbered more than 100,000 but today, less than 10,000 cheetahs remain, primarily in Africa. The knowledge that these spectacular animals could disappear within her lifetime has driven Dr. Marker to do all she can to save them, from establishing the most successful captive cheetah breeding program in North America to founding one of the top cheetah research and conservation groups in the world.

Laurie Marker grew up riding horses on her family's backyard farm in southern California. Her love for animals led her to spend all of her spare time working as a veterinary assistant. In college, she majored in agriculture, eventually earning her doctorate in zoology from England's Oxford University. When Laurie was just 20 years old, she began working at Wildlife Safari Park in Oregon as a veterinary technician. She met, and was captivated by, these stunning animals built for speed. A cheetah can go from 0 to 70 miles per hour (0–112 km/h) in four seconds. "I realized no one knew much about cheetahs, and that I wanted to know everything there was

(Opposite) Cheetah keeper Lacey Braun cuddles with a female cheetah cub at the Smithsonian Conservation Biology Institute in Front Royal, Virginia.

Labor of Love

Think you'd like to run your own conservation group? You'll need to be detail-oriented, a people person, and willing to hit the road. Dr. Laurie Marker travels the globe for three months out of each year, raising funds to keep her nonprofit conservation organization going. She also attends conferences to give lectures about CCF's work. When she's home in Namibia, her days are equally as full. In the morning, she usually meets with her staff to discuss the care of the livestock, dogs, and cheetahs housed at the facility. Some of the rescued and orphaned cheetahs are directly under her care, so she'll feed them and make sure their pens are clean. Her job also requires plenty of time at her desk. "I spend a lot of my time writing scientific papers, reviewing research data, making contacts with our supporters, and always trying to raise funds so we can continue to do our work," she says. "I am not sure I always love what I do, but I do what I must so what I love will survive."

to know about them," recalls Dr. Marker. "I focused my research on finding out more about this magnificent animal, and as I learned more about them, people from around the world asked me to share what I could with them." Soon, she was helping to develop a captive cheetah breeding program at the park. More than 100 cheetah cubs were born at Wildlife Safari in the fourteen years Dr. Marker was there.

Melody Taft of the Humane Society of the United States befriends a cheetah during her visit to an animal facility in Nairobi, Kenya.

As part of her studies, Dr. Marker went to Namibia, in Africa, home to the largest cheetah population on Earth. There she found that livestock ranchers considered cheetahs a threat to their livestock and were shooting them at the rate of 800 to 900 per year. Habitat loss, lack of genetic variation, high infant deaths, and disease were also taking their toll. To try to help turn things around, Dr. Marker moved to Namibia and founded Cheetah Conservation Fund (CCF). She traveled the countryside, talking to farmers and listening to their concerns. Then she showed them what her research revealed: cheetahs would rather hunt wild prey, but drought conditions had reduced prey levels and forced some cheetahs to kill livestock as an alternative food source. She also found

Wild cheetahs hitch a ride on the roof of a
Land Rover at Nairobi National Park in Kenya.

an innovative way to help ranchers protect their herds from cheetahs (as well
as other predators). In 1994, CCF began breeding livestock guard dogs at its
facility and providing them to local ranchers. The dogs were not trained to
attack but to bark and posture. A barking dog is usually enough of a deterrent
to scare away a cheetah or any other predator. Namibian farmers began to
see cheetahs in a new light and now share the land with their onetime foes.
Many even support tourism, which helps to boost the local economy.

Cheetah populations in Namibia have rebounded, but Dr. Marker says the work to protect these striking, swift cats is far from finished. Cheetahs live, and face threats, in as many as twenty-four countries. "I see hope for the future but also a short time in order to change the world so that cheetahs can survive into the future," says the conservationist, who has now rescued more than 800 cheetahs. "Each cheetah is special, amazingly beautiful, and worth trying to save."

Charismatic Creatures

After graduating from college with a bachelor of science in zoology, Amanda Vincent, who is Canadian, traveled through Europe, Asia, the Middle East, and Australia searching for her life's calling. "I took any interesting job I could find," she recalls, "from sheepshearing in the Australian outback to researching dugongs (sea cows) along the Australian coast."

Yet for all of her exciting experiences, it was a small, mysterious being of the sea that captured her heart and changed her life. "Seahorses are odd and fascinating creatures," says Dr. Vincent. "I was drawn to them because they are utterly unique among fishes and very little was known about them when I was starting out as a researcher." While earning her doctorate at the University of Cambridge in the United Kingdom, Dr. Vincent became fascinated by seahorse reproduction. Many seahorses mate for life. Also, they are the only known animal on Earth where the male of the species becomes pregnant. The female seahorse deposits her eggs in the pouch of the male seahorse where he fertilizes and nourishes them until it's time for them to hatch.

Dr. Vincent was the first biologist in the world to conduct an underwater study of seahorses. These petite masters of camouflage can change color to blend in with their surroundings, initially making it quite difficult for Dr. Vincent to find them. She got the hang of it, though, learning to search

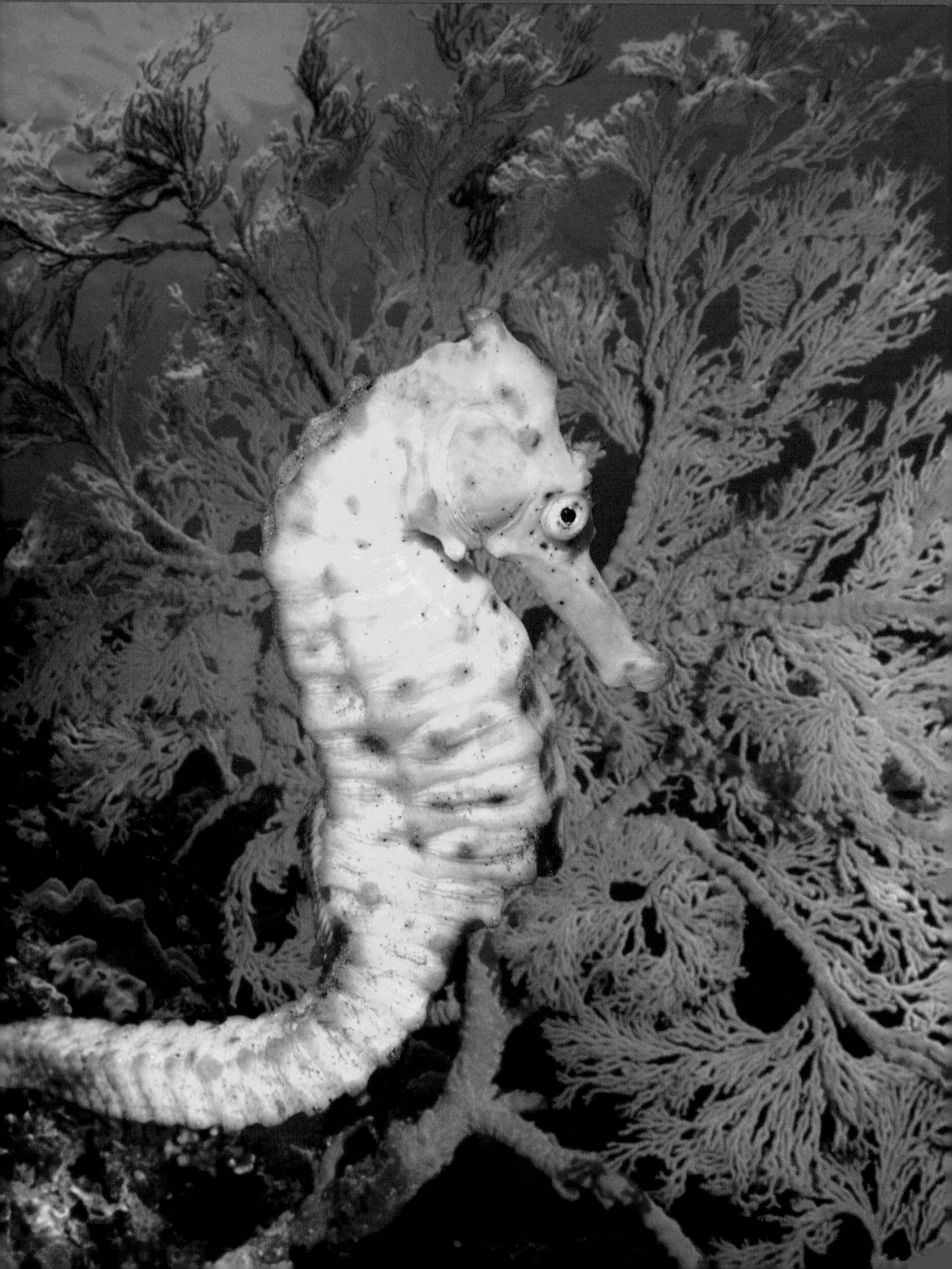

the grasses for their **prehensile** tails. Hour after hour, day after day, she observed seahorses in the wild and ended up logging more than 1,000 hours underwater for her doctoral dissertation!

Through her exhaustive research, Dr. Vincent was also the first scientist to discover that seahorses were in trouble.

Human interference, such as harvesting for decorative use in aquariums, has threatened the seahorses' existence. Seahorses are important to the ecosystem and removing or destroying them can be disruptive.

Tens of millions of the fish were being taken by humans every year for use in traditional medicines, aquarium displays, and as curiosities. By the early 1990s, it was clear to her that such overharvesting was not only jeopardizing seahorse populations but also damaging entire marine ecosystems. "Seahorses are a flagship species for marine conservation, charismatic symbols of the seagrasses, mangroves, coral reefs, estuaries, and seaweeds where they make their homes," explains Dr. Vincent. "Protecting seahorses means protecting these diverse habitats all of the marine life that lives therein."

In 1996, Dr. Vincent and colleague Dr. Heather Koldewey launched Project Seahorse, the first conservation group in the world to study and protect seahorses. The group also reaches out to cultures that depend on seahorse fishing to survive, to help them find a balance so that both seahorses and humans can flourish. Dr. Vincent says one of the highlights of her

(Opposite) The upright-swimming seahorse is found in shallow tropical and temperate waters throughout the world. They have no teeth and no stomach, and are among the only animal species on Earth in which the male bears the unborn young.

Be a Conservationist Now

In 2013, Project Seahorse launched a new website that allows anyone who spots a seahorse on an underwater dive to share their information with the conservation group. Dr. Vincent hopes that including the public in her organization's efforts will help fill in the gaps in current knowledge and improve seahorse conservation. To find out how you can get involved, log on to the Project Seahorse website.

career came in 2002, when Project Seahorse played a key role in generating a landmark global agreement under the Convention on the International Trade in Endangered Species, forbidding countries to export more seahorses than wild populations can handle. Additionally, the conservation organization helped create thirty-four marine-protected areas in Danajon Bank, Philippines, a rare and threatened double-barrier reef.

Dr. Vincent is one of the world's top experts on seahorses, yet says we have barely scratched the surface when it comes to our understanding of these charming creatures. "Many species are listed as 'Data Deficient' because we simply do not know enough about their conservation status," she explains. "We need more seahorse researchers and we need more documentation generally about seahorse sightings."

As for the next generation of conservationists who will follow in her footsteps, Dr. Vincent says, "Education is important, but you also need to get out there in the world and experience new cultures and environments if your goal is to make a difference. After I completed my travels, I knew I wanted to help secure a future for our oceans. This has become my life's work, and I love it. You need to find something you love to do, and dedicate yourself to it. It won't always be easy, and sometimes it will even be grueling, but if you do what you love, it will be worthwhile."

(Opposite) A scuba diver observes a long-snouted seahorse.

FIVE

On the Horizon

In about the time that it has taken you to read this book so far, scientists figure another plant or animal species on Earth has gone extinct. That's a loss of more than 26,000 species each year. Extinction is part of the natural order of life, but according to The International Union for Conservation of Nature (IUCN), the current rate of species extinction is between 1,000 and 10,000 times higher than normal. The blame falls primarily on humanity's shoulders. The IUCN cites climate change, habitat destruction, pollution, overfishing and hunting, and the introduction of nonnative species as the biggest threats facing wildlife. Scientists say the problem will only continue to grow along with our human population, which has already surged past 7 billion worldwide and is projected to reach 10 billion by the end of this century.

What does this trend mean for those who plan to enter the field of wildlife conservation? In the future, more zoologists and wildlife biologists will be needed to study the effects of population growth and development on wildlife and their habitats, according to the U.S. Department of Labor. The agency says demand is also expected to be strong for those who research, create, and execute conservation plans to combat the threats that endanger wildlife and the nation's natural resources. "We think the ocean and sky is so

(Opposite) The elephants' stages of life are similar to those of humans. They form deep emotional bonds and have the ability to express a variety of emotions. This is part of the reasons why elephant conservationists find researching the animals' lives fascinating.

The last-known Tasmanian tiger was said to have died in 1936 while in captivity in a zoo located in the Tasmanian capital of Hobart. Some people remain convinced that the tiger still exists, often making claims to have seen them.

vast that our resources will never go away, but with more and more humans on Earth we need to recognize the planet has limits," explains Carey Stanton, senior director of the Education for National Wildlife Federation. "As our population grows, we're going to need to better manage our resources. The need for entomologists, ornithologists, and other specialized fields is going to expand. We're also going to need more people in the area of wildlife management, simply because the more we encroach on animal habitats the more encounters we're going to have with wildlife." Globally, as wildlife habitats are destroyed for farming and urban development, experts say conservationists will be essential in the areas of habitat preservation and restoration, and education. Specialists in animal diseases, **toxicology**, and

Optimistic Outlook

Thanks to aging baby boomers, who are starting to retire, the U.S. Fish and Wildlife Service predicts it will have more jobs available for young people in the near future. A survey of the agency's National Wildlife Refuge employees found 43 percent of those surveyed plan to retire by 2020. The United States has 533 wildlife refuges (at least one in every state and territory), employing about 3,000 people. The refuge system provides 150 million acres of habitat for more than 750 animal and plant species.

Students attending the FIS3200 Stream Habitat Measurement Techniques course at the U.S. Fish and Wildlife Service's National Conservation Training Center, practice using a sight level for mapping profiles of various habitat features.

wildlife diversity (genetics) will be also critically important in helping animal populations recover.

Despite these needs, experts say the job market overall is, and will continue to be, competitive. Wildlife conservation is a popular career choice. More people are drawn to the profession than there are jobs available. Many nonprofit conservation organizations have small staffs with a limited number

A Fiery Spirit

Primate researcher Dr. Dian Fossey was a passionate conservationist who devoted her life to putting a spotlight on the plight of the endangered mountain gorilla. Her 1983 book, *Gorillas in the Mist*, chronicled her time spent studying and living among the mountain gorillas in the Republic of Congo and Rwanda. She shared the threats these intelligent animals faced from poachers and African government officials seeking to turn the gorillas' habitat into farmlands. Two years after her book was published and became a best seller, Fossey was murdered in Rwanda. Although some speculate the poachers she fought so hard to oppose were responsible, the case was never solved. A movie based on her book was made in 1988. Today, The Dian Fossey Gorilla Fund International continues its founder's mission to protect the 790 mountain gorillas left in the wild.

of full-time positions. Also, if a group is based overseas, say, working in Africa or Asia, many of those jobs are likely to go to local residents. Yet, there are things you can to do ensure you are well prepared to enter the job market and that will give you an edge over the competition when you do. First, get a solid education in the sciences. Pursue advanced degrees as your schedule and finances allow. Next, seek out volunteer and internship opportunities to work in nature or with animals whenever possible. You'll not only gain valuable experience, but it could lead to a permanent job. Also, don't limit yourself. Explore a full range of options. Consider a career working on behalf of a species people are less familiar with than, say, pandas, polar bears, or dolphins. You might find your niche helping seahorses, bats, caracals, bonobos, okapi, saiga, fossas, or one of the other thousands of animals that appear on the IUCN's red list, meaning those that are most at risk of extinction. Finally, conservation work can be challenging, so it's important your heart is in it. Choose a path that intrigues you and fuels your passion. "If you have a fascination, follow it," advises Dr. John French, the conservationist you met at the beginning of this book. "You'll never be happy making money if what you do is boring and uninteresting to you."

The Path Ahead

Clearly our planet needs wildlife conservationists in the years to come. But the challenge comes in financially supporting these efforts. Can we do it? Will we want to? Conservation efforts typically rely on funding from public and/or private sources. The nation's recent economic slump has forced state and federal conservation agencies to tighten their belts. Many nonprofit conservation groups, who rely on private donations to survive, have had to do the same. For some it means hiring fewer new employees, not replacing employees who leave, or even cutting full-time positions to part-time. The U.S. Department of Labor predicts employment for biologists and zoologists to grow by only about 7 percent between now and 2020, slower than the average for all other occupations.

For people to make funding conservation a priority, they must first recognize its significance. Yet experts say as televisions, computers, telephones, and video games keep more of us indoors, we are gradually losing touch with the natural world. "As you get less and less experience with nature, your desire to protect it decreases because you don't see why it is relevant to your day-to-day life," says National Wildlife Federation's Carey Stanton. "Wetlands are not just important to frogs and fishes, but they provide many benefits to people, such as filtering water, determining whether or not we have flooding, and recreation. Outdoor experiences are so important, because they connect us with resources and wildlife. That doesn't mean you have to go out in your hip waders in a wetland. Go on a nature walk in your neighborhood. Play on the beach. You are more likely to protect something when you know it and care about it."

Despite our indoor habits, Americans do seem to be getting the message. A 2012 Nature Conservancy poll found that 87 percent of Americans agree that state and national parks, forests, monuments, and wildlife areas are an essential part of their state's quality of life. Four out of five citizens said they would be willing to pay additional taxes to protect the nation's land, water, and wildlife.

There is no doubt that, even with healthy funding, future wildlife conservationists have plenty of work ahead of them. The IUCN reports nearly one-third of amphibians, more than one in eight birds, and nearly a quarter of mammals are threatened with extinction. Some figures report as much as 30 percent of Earth's lifeforms could be on the road to disappearing forever within the next century. In the face of such odds, it can be a daunting task trying to change things. Yet there are those who are willing to devote their entire lives toward that goal. Could you be one of them?

On the Horizon

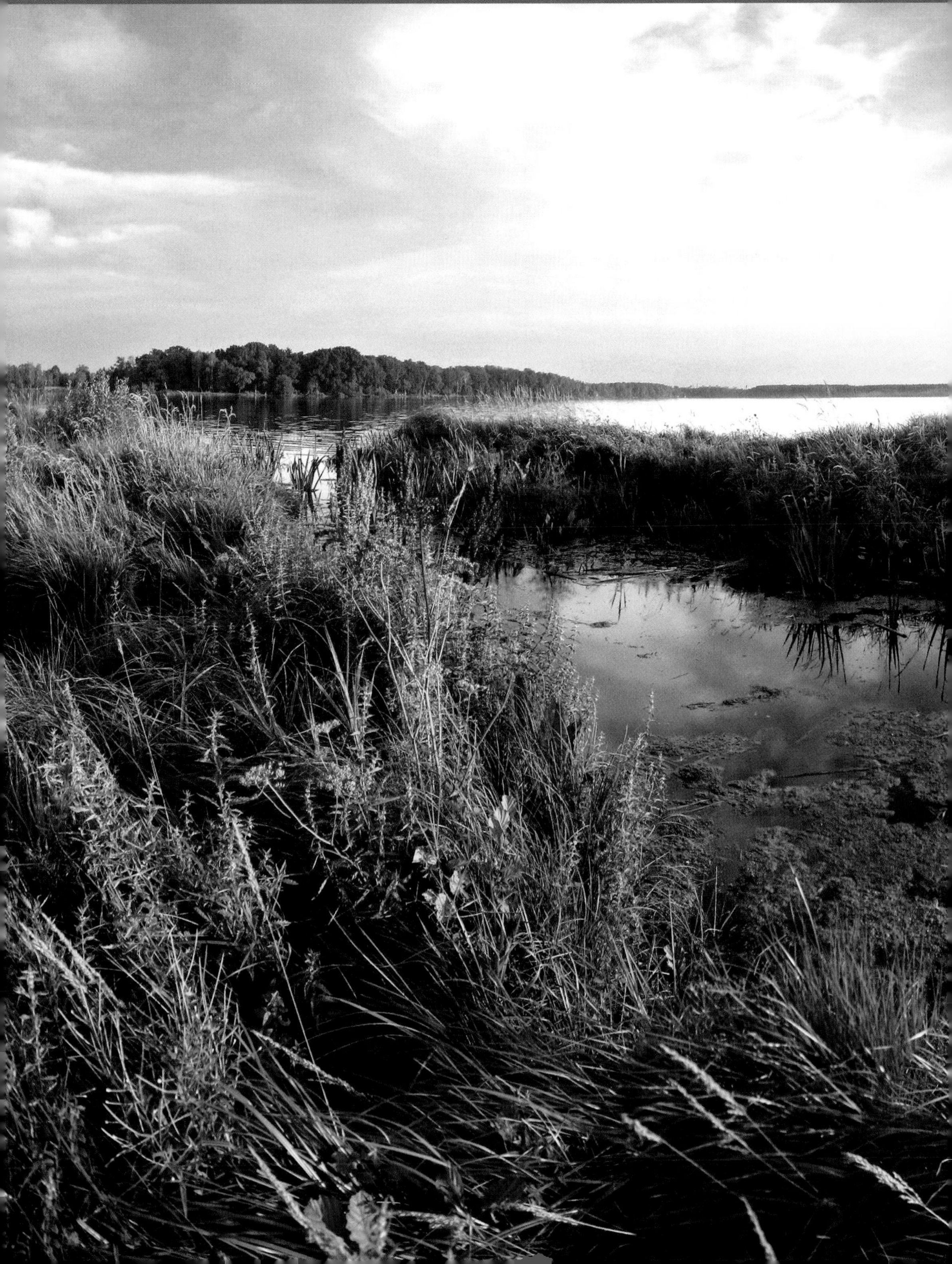

Glossary

anesthetize	to render insensitive or unconscious through the administration of drugs
biology	the science of life or living matter
camera traps	remote digital cameras that are activated by heat or motion
ecology	the branch of biology concerning the relationship between living organisms and their environment, including other organisms
endangered	in conservation, an animal that is likely to become extinct in the near future
extinction	no longer in existence
field research	a scientific study conducted in person in a natural setting
genetics	the branch of biology concerning heredity and variation in organisms

internships	paid or unpaid student programs in a professional workplace, in which students receive college credit in return for their work
marine biology	the science of organisms that live in, or are dependent upon, the ocean
nonprofit	not established for the purpose of making money
poachers	people who trespass to fish or hunt animals illegally
prehensile	the ability to grasp or take hold of something
species	a class of individual life-forms having some common characteristics or qualities
thesis	an independent, original research project; also called a dissertation
threatened	in conservation, a species that is likely to become endangered in the near future
toxicology	the branch of science concerned with poisons and their effects
zoology	the branch of biology dealing with animals

Find Out More

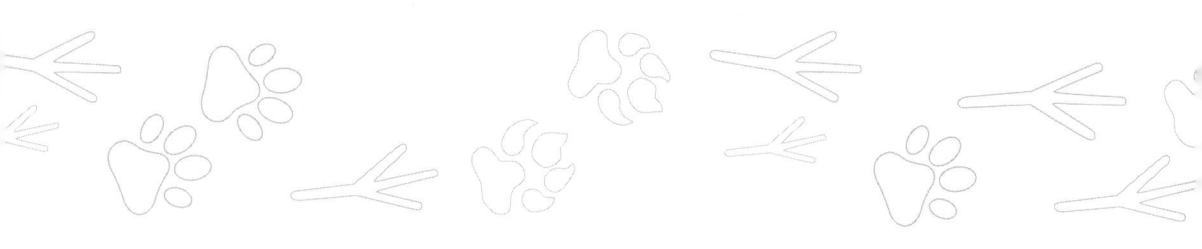

Books

Field, Shelly. *Career Opportunities: Working with Animals*. New York: Checkmark Books, 2012.

Ryan-Flynn, Mary Susan. *What Can I Do Now? Animal Careers*. New York: Ferguson, 2010.

Scardina, Julie and Jeff Flocken. *Wildlife Heroes: 40 Leading Conservationists and the Animals They are Committed to Saving*. Philadelphia, PA: Running Press, 2012.

Websites

National Wildlife Federation (NWF)

www.nwf.org

At the nation's largest member-supported conservation organization, learn about the issues facing wildlife and see how you can get involved. You can also find out more about NWF volunteer opportunities, internships, and fellowships.

U.S. Fish and Wildlife Service (FWS)

www.fws.gov

Log on to view the FWS Threatened and Endangered Species List. Read about job opportunities and internships with FWS, as well as the Youth Conservation Corps summer job program for teens.

The Wildlife Society

www.wildlife.org

This nonprofit organization is comprised of career professionals that manage, conserve, and study wildlife populations and habitats. Posted on their website, you'll find career information, a list of colleges with student chapters, and hands-on opportunities for college students.

Index

About the Author

Trudi Strain Trueit is the author of more than eighty fiction and nonfiction books for young readers. A former television journalist and weather forecaster, she enjoys writing about career exploration, health, weather, earth science, and history. Look for her other titles in the Careers with Animals series: *Animal Trainer*, *Animal Physical Therapist*, and *Veterinarian*. Trueit has a bachelor's degree in broadcast journalism and lives in Everett, Washington, with her husband and their two cats. Read more about Trueit and her books at www.truditrueit.com.